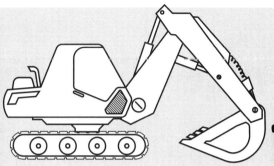

The Cars, Trucks, Trains, and Planes Pre-K Workbook

Celeste Meiergerd

Published in the United States by:
Ulysses Press
P.O. Box 3440
Berkeley, CA 94703
www.ulyssespress.com

ISBN: 978-1-64604-038-4
Library of Congress Control Number: 2020931849

Printed in Canada by Marquis Book Printing
10 9 8 7 6 5 4 3 2 1

Acquisitions editor: Claire Sielaff
Managing editor: Claire Chun
Editor: Julie Holland
Proofreader: Renee Rutledge
Front cover design: Tobi Carter
Cover art: plane, car, train © IrynMerry/shutterstock.com; excavator © Aohodesign/
    shutterstock.com
Interior design and layout: what!design @ whatweb.com
Interior art: shutterstock.com

Contents

Chapter 1

Line Tracing

Trace the line to help the race car cross the finish line.

FINISH

Trace the lines to help the emergency vehicles get to the city in time to help.

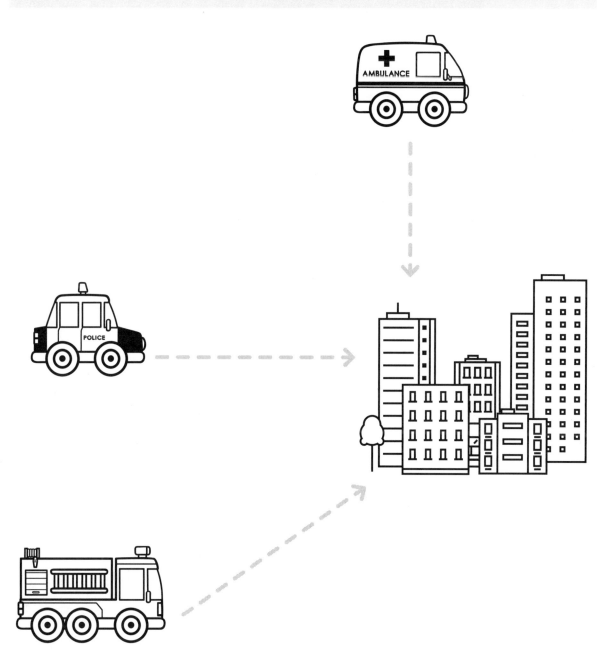

Trace the line so that the boat can make it to the water.

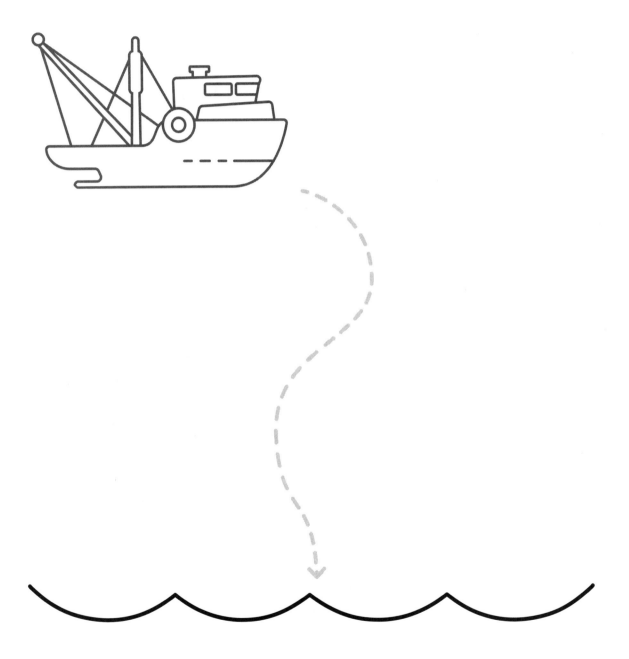

The Cars, Trucks, Trains, and Planes Pre-K Workbook

Connect the train cars to get the train back on the tracks.

Trace the line so that the helicopter flies up above the city.

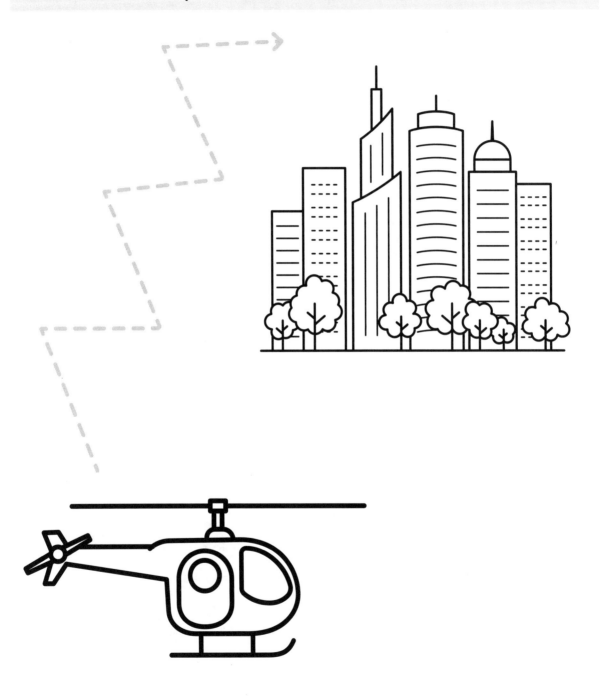

Help the cranes reach their construction sites.

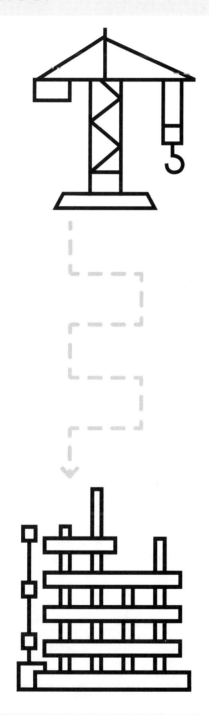

Pave the street with the concrete mixer truck by following the path to the road.

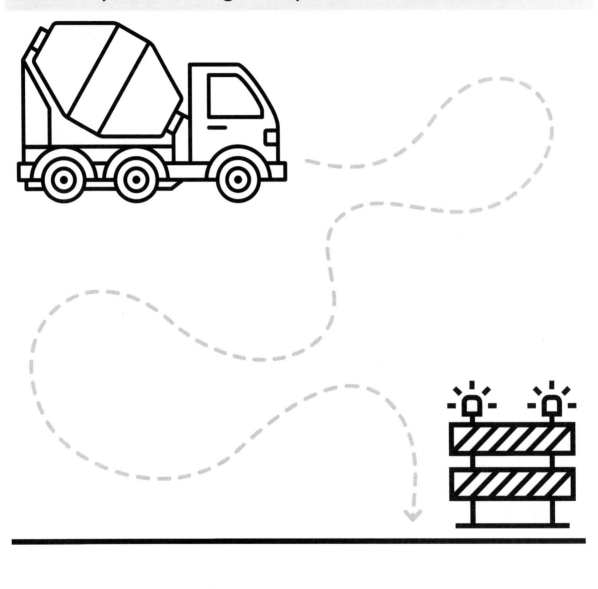

The Cars, Trucks, Trains, and Planes Pre-K Workbook

Move the excavators to the cement mixers by following the paths below.

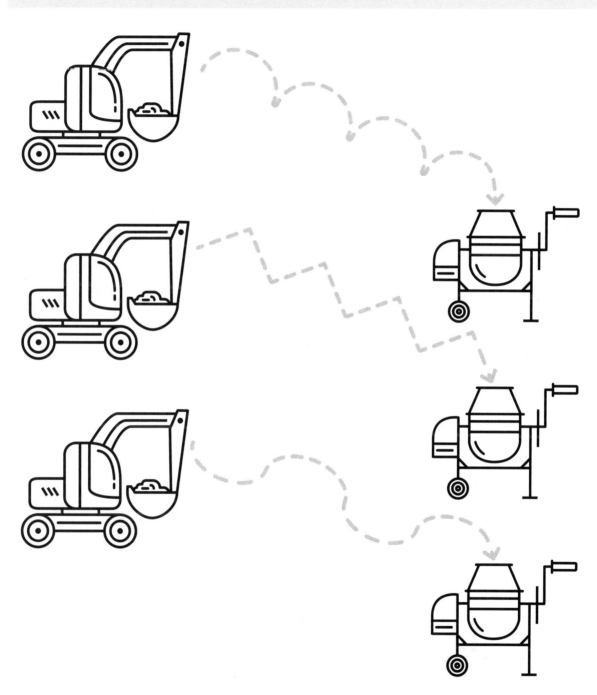

Trace the lines from the wheels so the dump truck can be on its way.

Land the airplane safely by following the path to the runway.

Chapter 2

Practice with Scissors

Cut on the dotted lines from the airplane and the helicopter to help them get above the city.

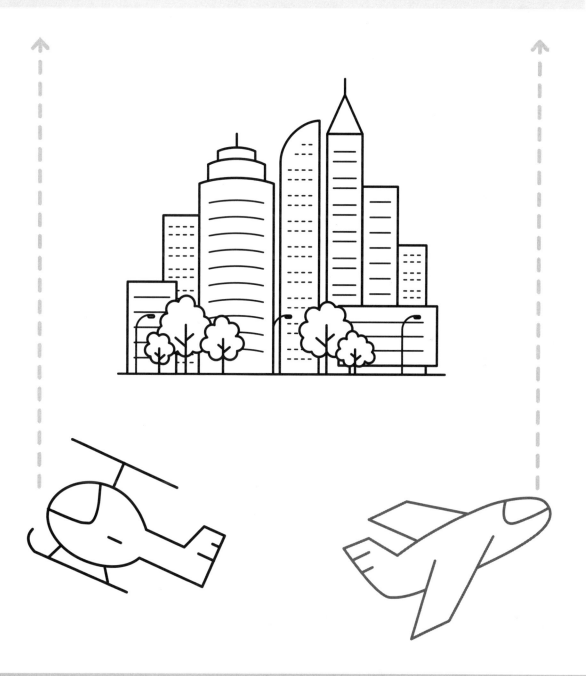

Cut around the obstacles for the car to make it to the finish line.

Cut on the dotted lines to help the construction workers get to their bulldozers.

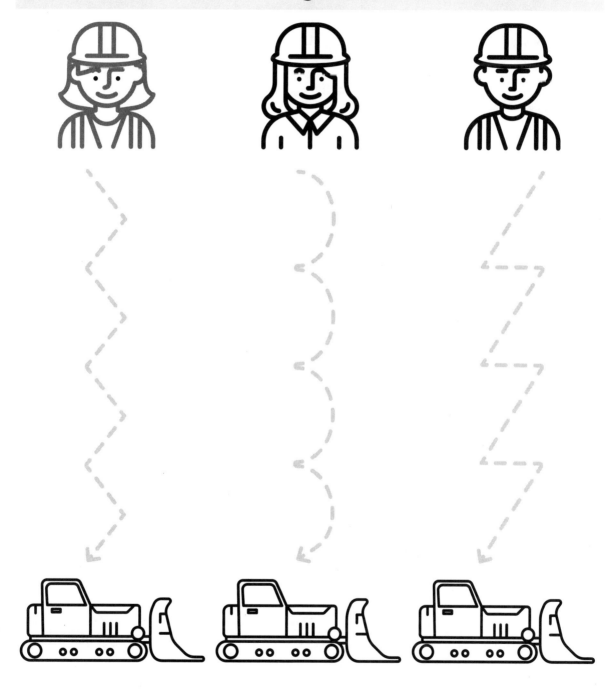

Cut the dotted line waves to keep the boat on course.

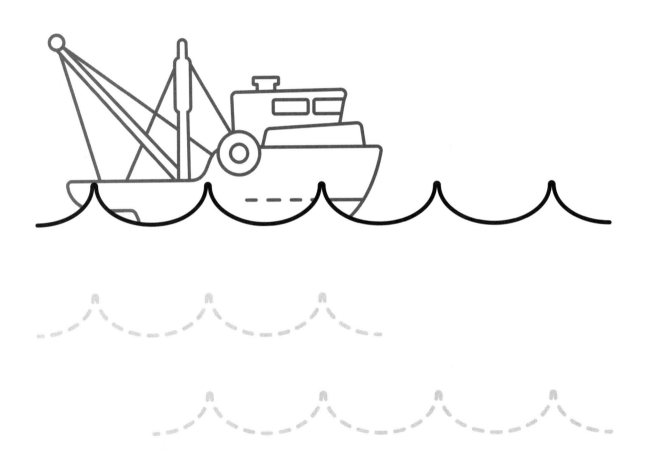

The Cars, Trucks, Trains, and Planes Pre-K Workbook

Uh-oh! There are mountains blocking these trains from their routes! **Cut** the dotted-line mountains to help the trains get back to their tracks.

The car got a flat tire in the city! **Cut** around the tire to remove it.

The Cars, Trucks, Trains, and Planes Pre-K Workbook

Help the tractor plow the field. **Cut** the tractor's path out on the dotted lines.

Cut the dotted line from the fire truck's crane to the tree to save the cat that is stuck inside!

The Cars, Trucks, Trains, and Planes Pre-K Workbook

Follow the path and **cut** the dotted line to help the car get around the construction on the road.

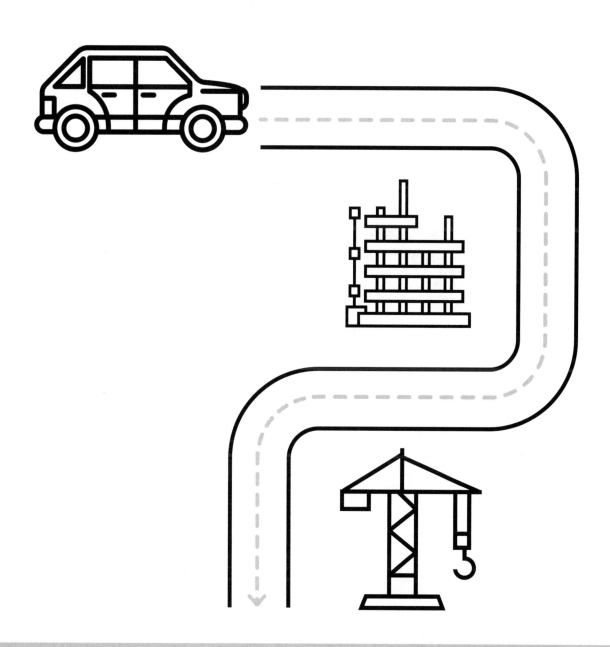

Cut out the car below to make your own vehicle to play with. Attach your car to a block with tape so it can stand on its own.

Chapter 3

Letter Tracing and Recognition

A is for Airplane

Trace the uppercase letter **A** below. Follow the numbered arrows.

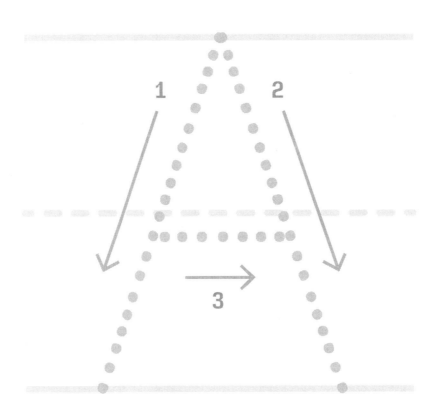

B is for Boat

Trace the uppercase letter **B** below. Follow the numbered arrows.

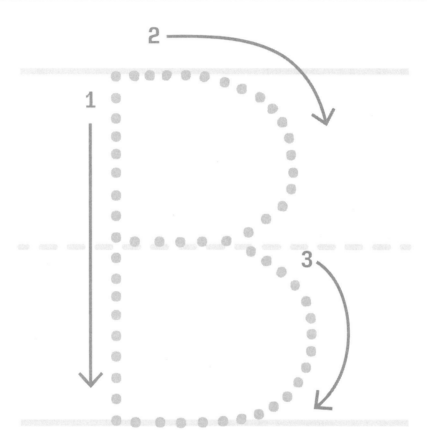

C is for Car

Trace the uppercase letter **C** below. Follow the numbered arrow.

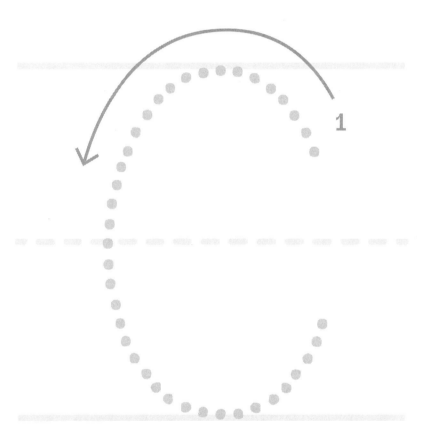

D is for Dump truck

Trace the uppercase letter **D** below. Follow the numbered arrows.

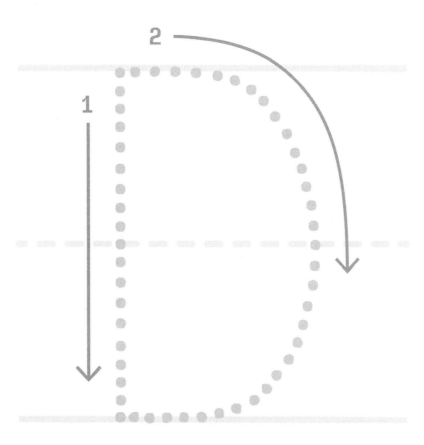

E is for Excavator

Trace the uppercase letter **E** below. Follow the numbered arrows.

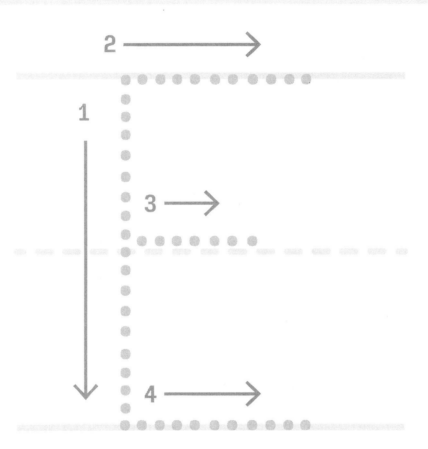

F is for Fire truck

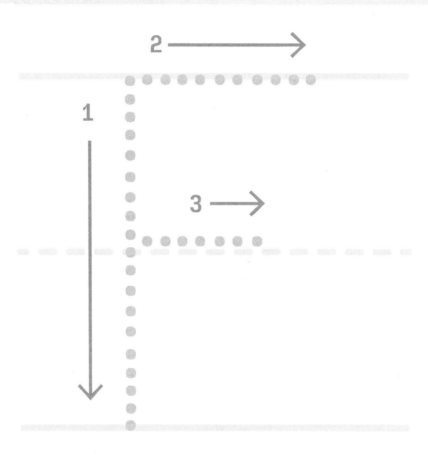

G is for Garbage truck

Trace the uppercase letter **G** below. Follow the numbered arrows.

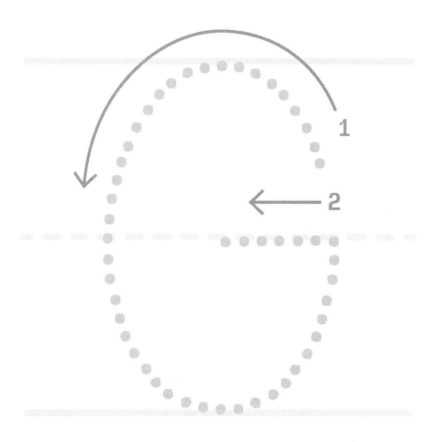

H is for Helicopter

Trace the uppercase letter **H** below. Follow the numbered arrows.

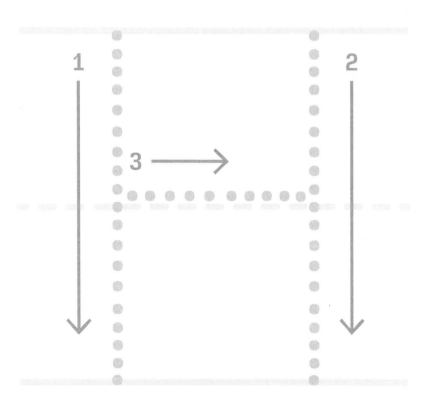

I is for Icebreaker

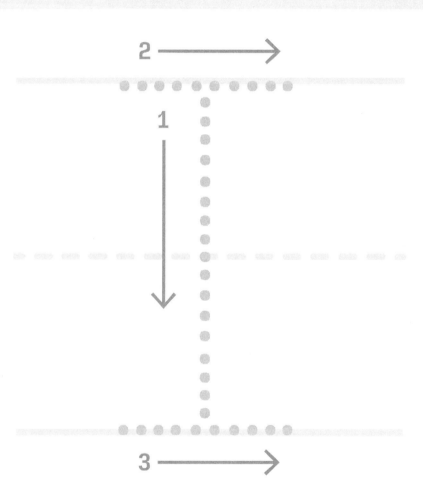

The Cars, Trucks, Trains, and Planes Pre-K Workbook

J is for Jet

Trace the uppercase letter **J** below. Follow the numbered arrows.

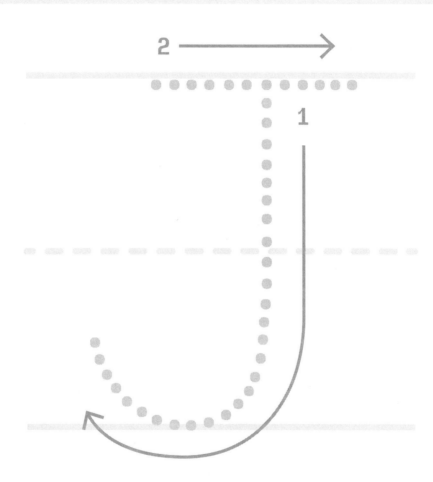

K is for Kayak

Trace the uppercase letter **K** below. Follow the numbered arrows.

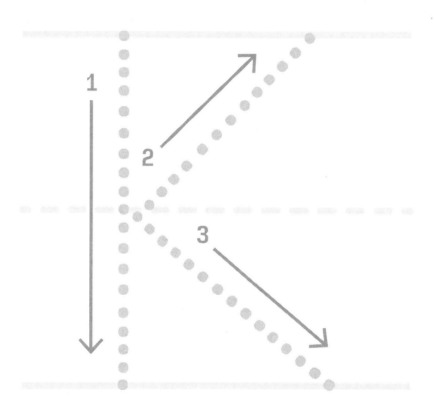

L is for Locomotive

Trace the uppercase letter **L** below. Follow the numbered arrows.

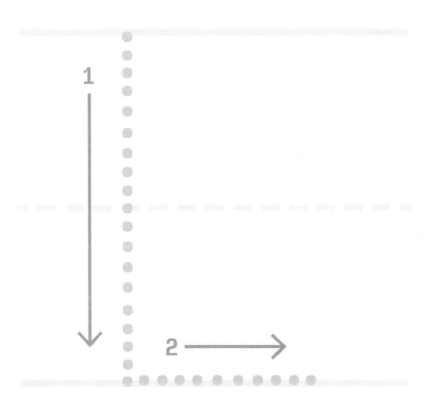

M is for Motorcycle

Trace the uppercase letter **M** below. Follow the numbered arrows.

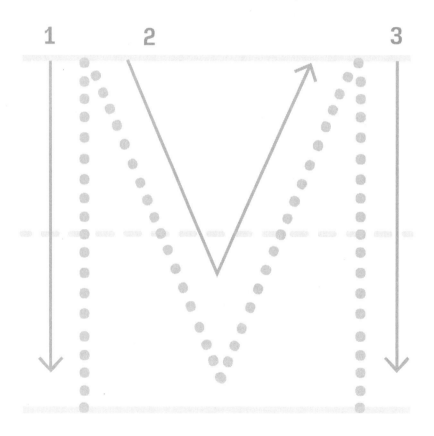

N is for Narrowboat

Trace the uppercase letter **N** below. Follow the numbered arrows.

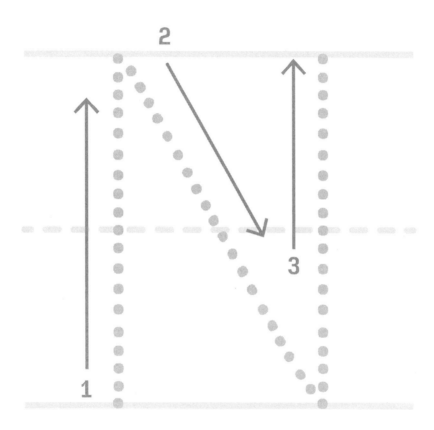

O is for Ocean liner

Trace the uppercase letter **O** below. Follow the numbered arrow.

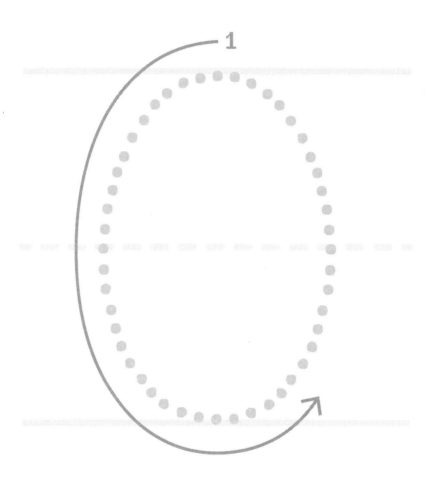

The Cars, Trucks, Trains, and Planes Pre-K Workbook

P is for Police car

Trace the uppercase letter **P** below. Follow the numbered arrows.

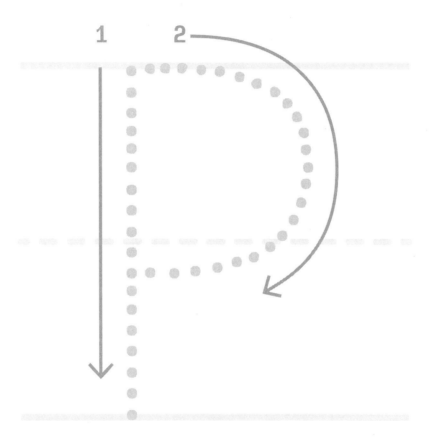

Q is for Quad bike

Trace the uppercase letter **Q** below. Follow the numbered arrows.

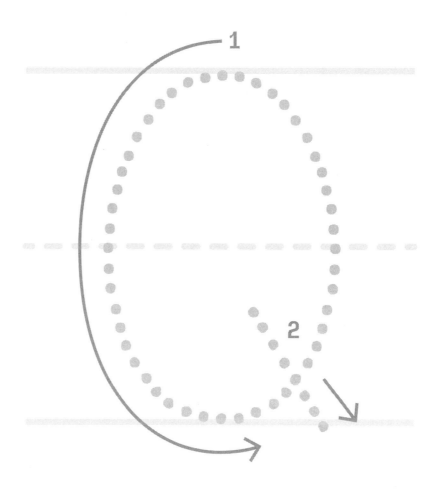

R is for Rocket ship

Trace the uppercase letter **R** below. Follow the numbered arrows.

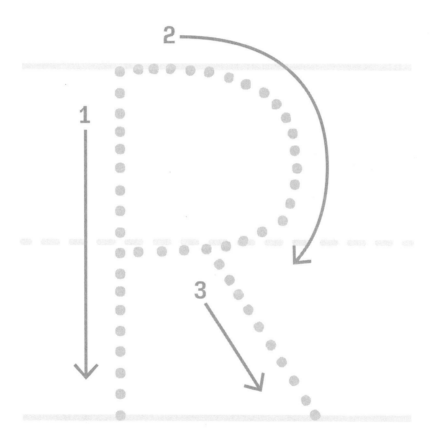

S is for Submarine

Trace the uppercase letter **S** below. Follow the numbered arrow.

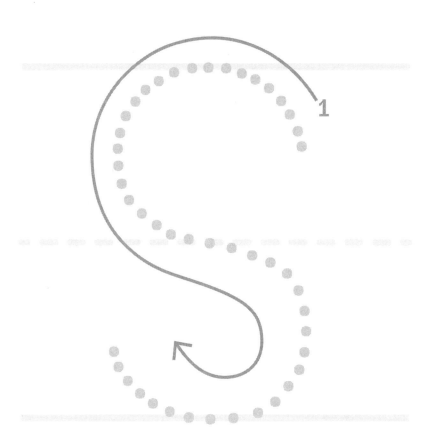

T is for Tram

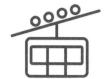

Trace the uppercase letter **T** below. Follow the numbered arrows.

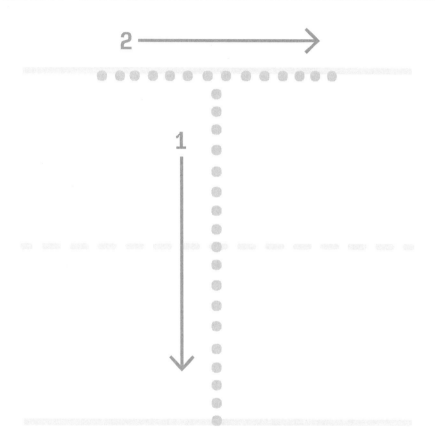

U is for Unicycle

Trace the uppercase letter **U** below. Follow the numbered arrow.

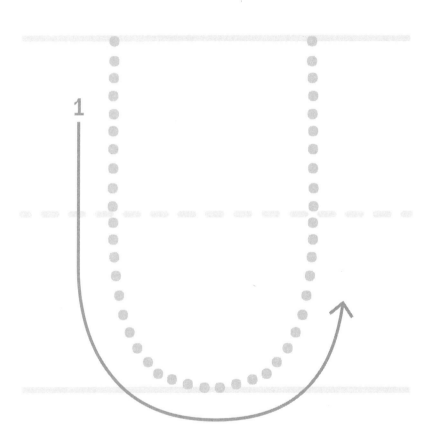

V is for Van

Trace the uppercase letter **V** below. Follow the numbered arrows.

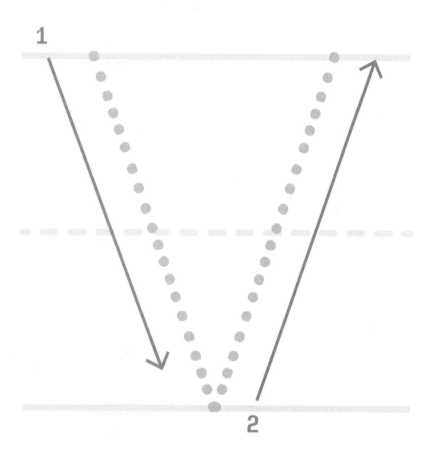

W is for Wheelbarrow

Trace the uppercase letter **W** below. Follow the numbered arrows.

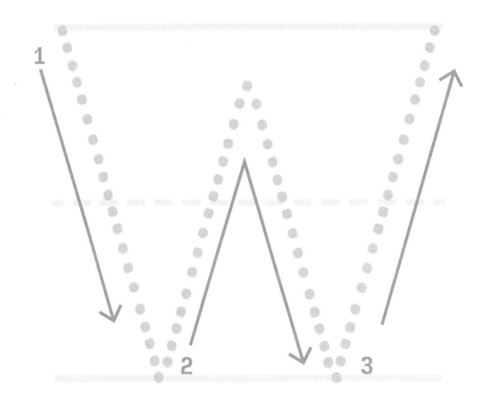

X is for Xebec

Trace the uppercase letter **X** below. Follow the numbered arrows.

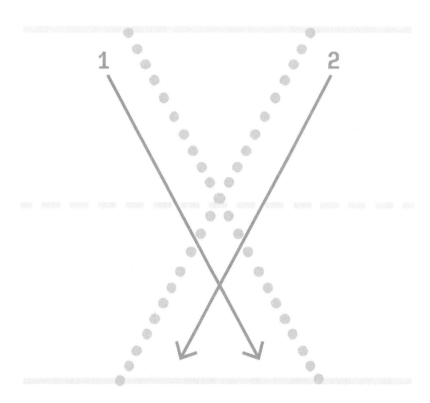

Y is for Yacht

Trace the uppercase letter **Y** below. Follow the numbered arrows.

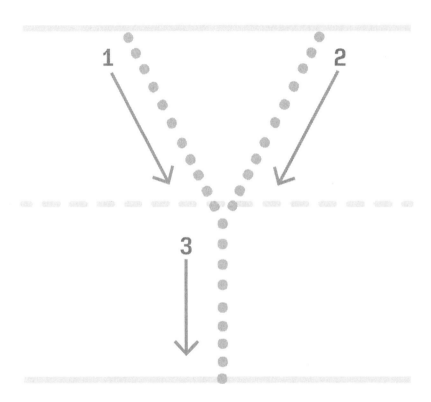

Z is for Zeppelin

Trace the uppercase letter **Z** below. Follow the numbered arrows.

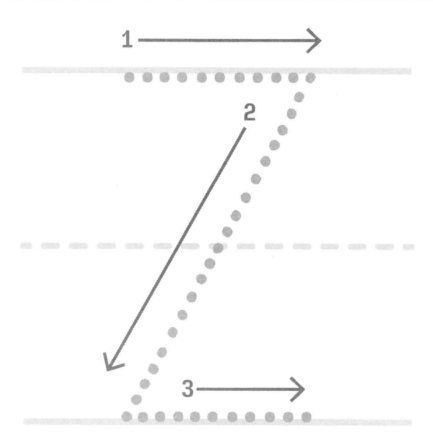

Aa

Trace the lowercase letter **a**. Follow the numbered arrows.

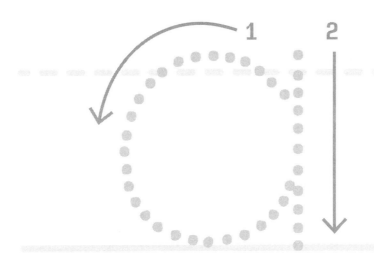

The Cars, Trucks, Trains, and Planes Pre-K Workbook

Bb

Trace the lowercase letter **b**. Follow the numbered arrows.

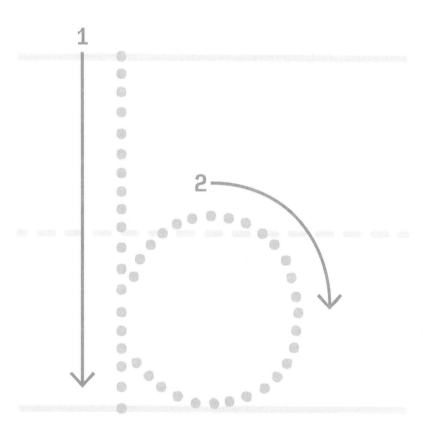

Cc

Trace the lowercase letter **c**. Follow the numbered arrow.

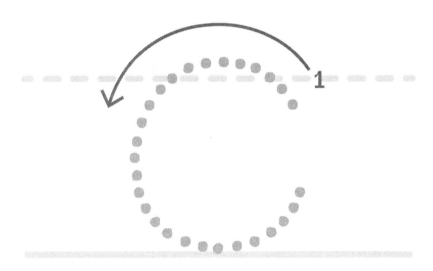

Dd

Trace the lowercase letter **d**. Follow the numbered arrows.

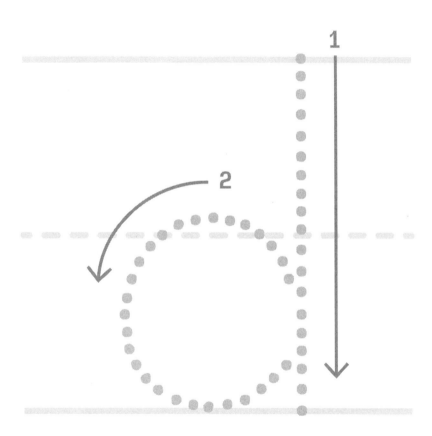

Ee

Trace the lowercase letter **e**. Follow the numbered arrows.

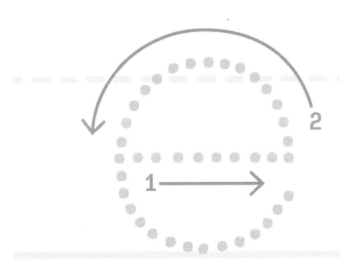

Ff

Trace the lowercase letter **f**. Follow the numbered arrows.

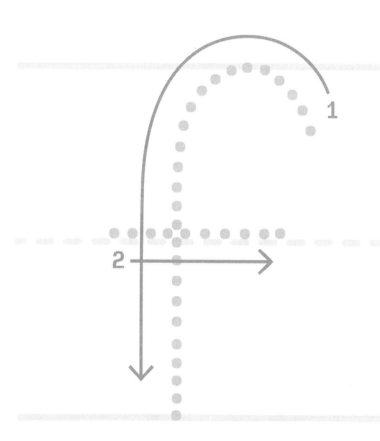

Gg

Trace the lowercase letter **g**. Follow the numbered arrows.

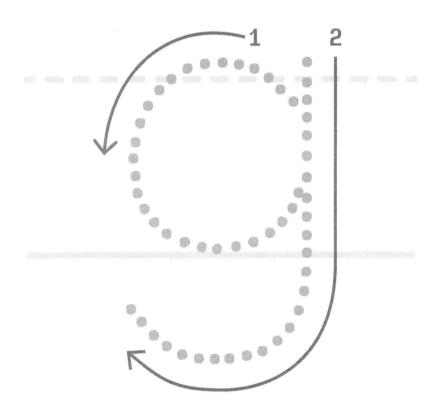

The Cars, Trucks, Trains, and Planes Pre-K Workbook

Hh

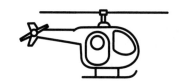

Trace the lowercase letter **h**. Follow the numbered arrows.

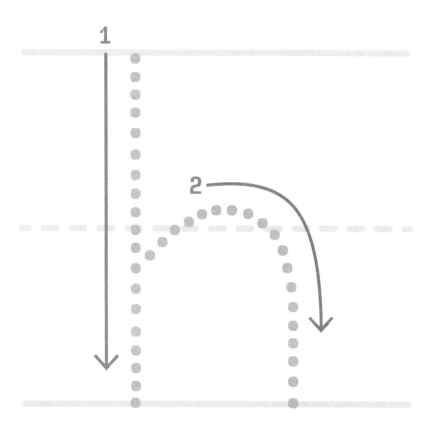

Ii

Trace the lowercase letter **i**. Follow the numbered arrow then dot the letter.

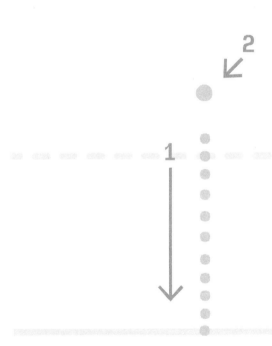

Jj

Trace the lowercase letter **j**. Follow the numbered arrow then dot the letter.

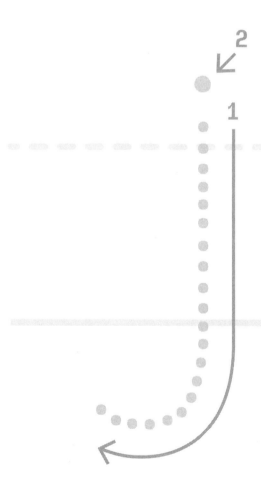

Kk

Trace the lowercase letter **k**. Follow the numbered arrows.

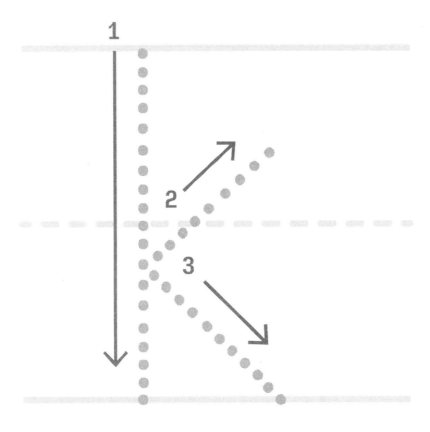

Ll

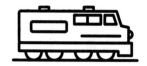

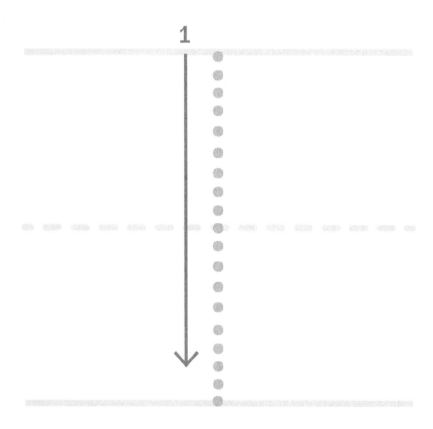

Mm

Trace the lowercase letter **m**. Follow the numbered arrows.

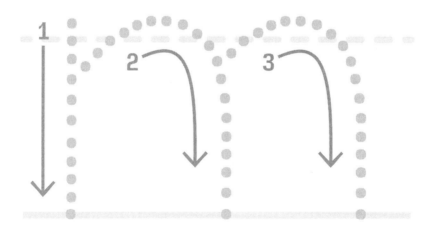

Nn

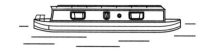

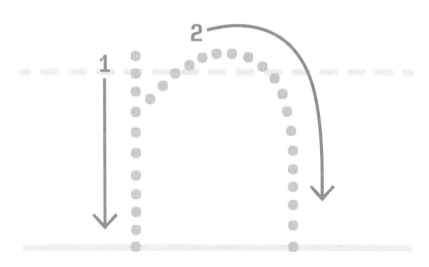

Oo

Trace the lowercase letter **o**. Follow the numbered arrow.

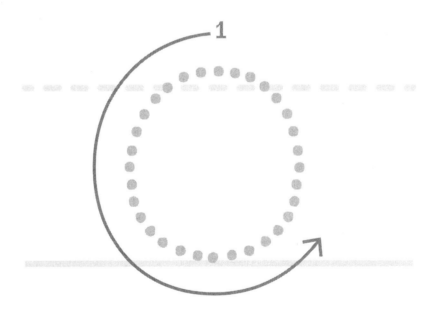

Pp

Trace the lowercase letter **p**. Follow the numbered arrows.

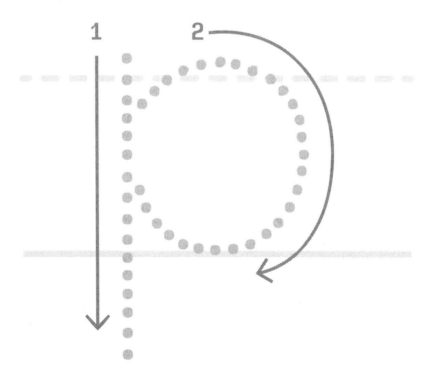

Qq

Trace the lowercase letter **q**. Follow the numbered arrows.

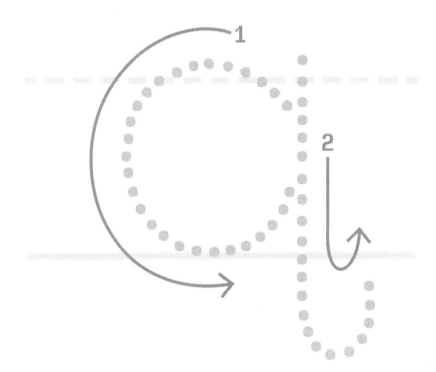

Rr

Trace the lowercase letter **r**. Follow the numbered arrows.

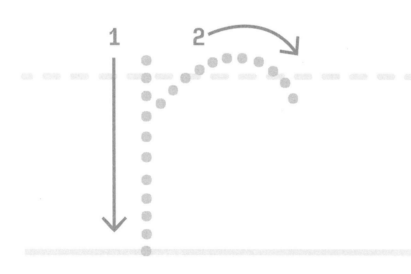

Ss

Trace the lowercase letter **s**. Follow the numbered arrow.

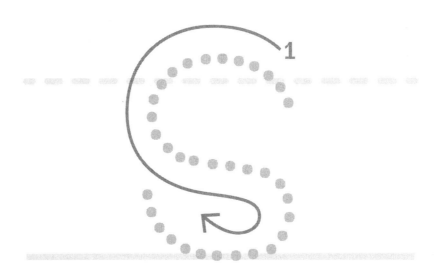

Tt

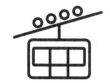

Trace the lowercase letter **t**. Follow the numbered arrows.

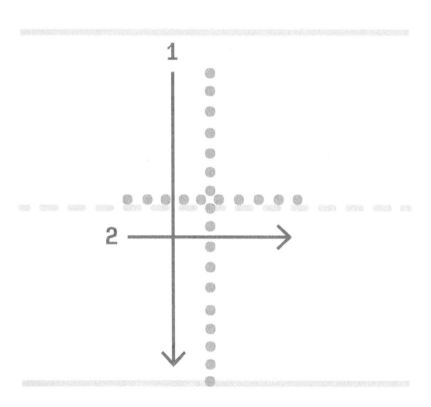

Uu

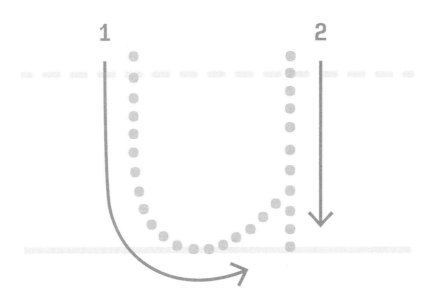

Vv

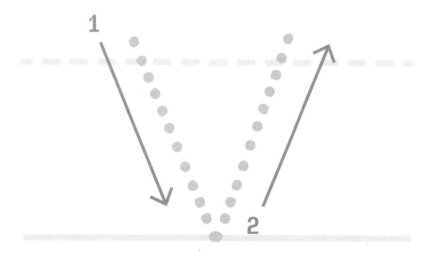

Ww

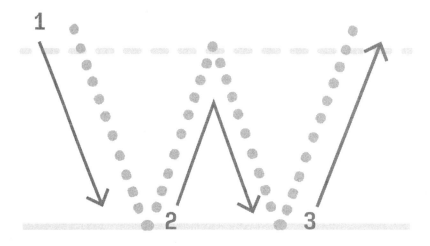

Xx

Trace the lowercase letter **x**. Follow the numbered arrows.

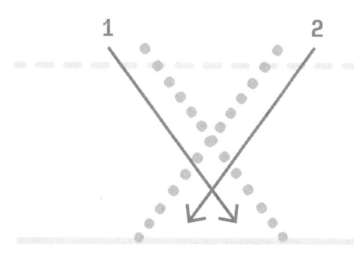

Yy

Trace the lowercase letter **y**. Follow the numbered arrows.

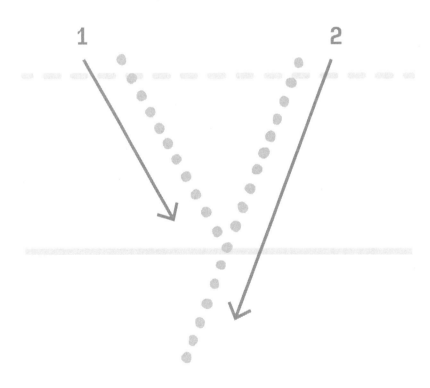

The Cars, Trucks, Trains, and Planes Pre-K Workbook

Zz

Trace the lowercase letter **z**. Follow the numbered arrows.

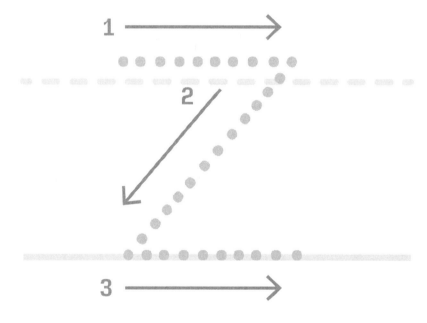

Chapter 4

Number Tracing and Identification

Trace and **write** the number **1**.

Trace

Write

1 trolley

The Cars, Trucks, Trains, and Planes Pre-K Workbook

Trace the word **one**.

one

Color **one** of the trucks below.

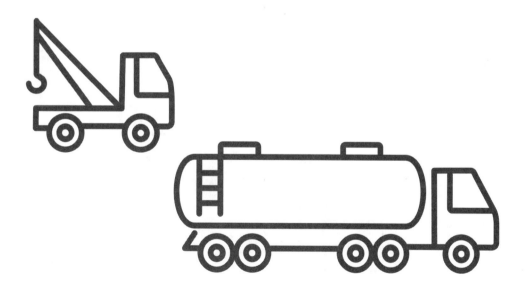

Trace and **write** the number **2**.

Trace

Write

2 wheels

Trace the word **two.**

Color **two** of the wheels on the fire truck.

Trace and **write** the number **3**.

Trace   Write

3 emergency vehicles

Trace the word **three**.

Color **three** of the train cars.

Trace and **write** the number **4**.

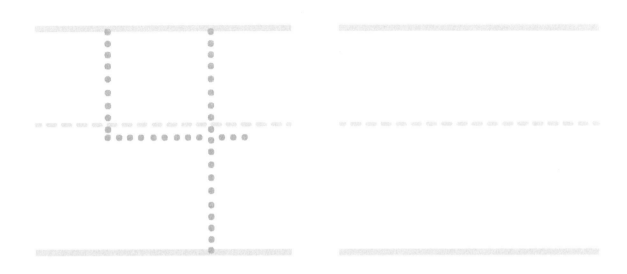

Trace   Write

4 bulldozers

Trace the word **four.**

Circle **four** of the windows on the boat.

Trace and **write** the number **5**.

Trace   Write

5 tall buildings

The Cars, Trucks, Trains, and Planes Pre-K Workbook

Trace the word **five**.

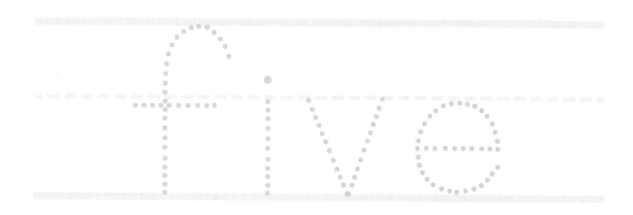

Circle **five** of the airplanes.

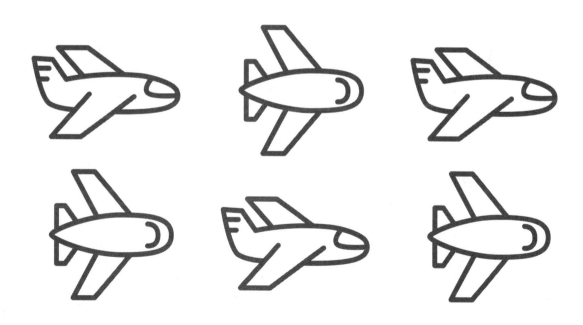

Trace and **write** the number **6**.

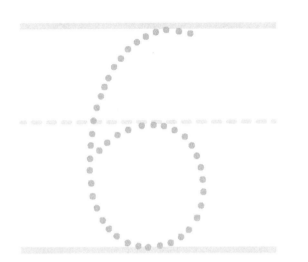

Trace   Write

6 taxis

The Cars, Trucks, Trains, and Planes Pre-K Workbook

Trace the word **six.**

six

Draw **six** boxes in the train cars.

Trace and **write** the number **7**.

Trace

Write

7 boats

Trace the word **seven.**

Draw seven cars on the road.

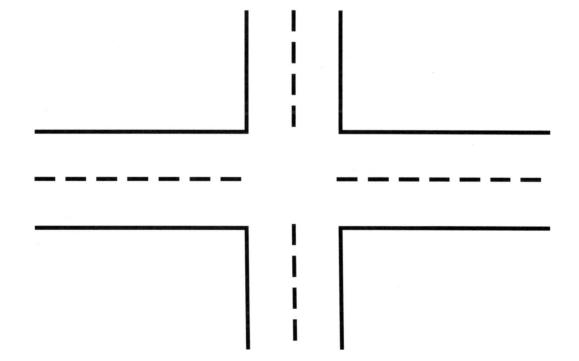

Trace and **write** the number **8**.

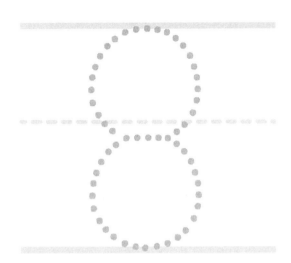

Trace   Write

8 helicopters

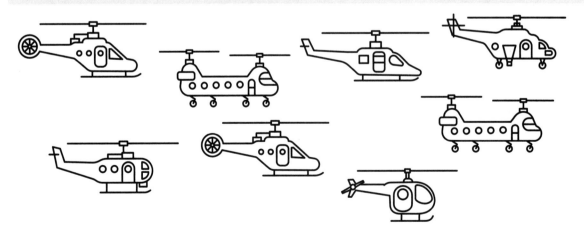

Trace the word **eight**.

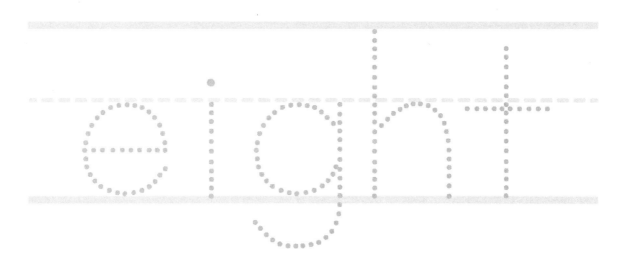

Draw **eight** logs for the crane to pick up.

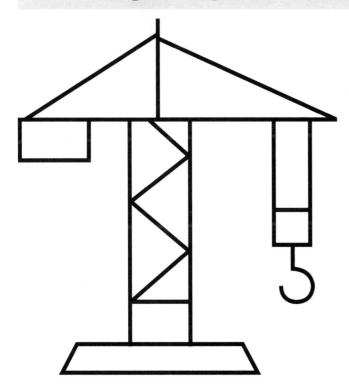

Trace and **write** the number **9**.

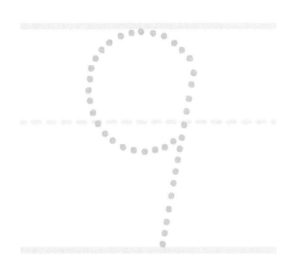

Trace   Write

9 boxes being moved

Trace the word **nine.**

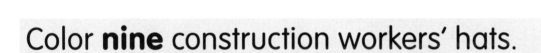

Color **nine** construction workers' hats.

Trace and **write** the number **10**.

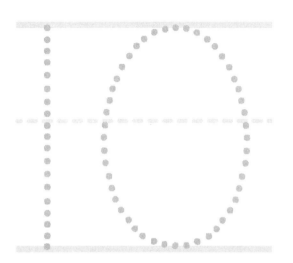

Trace   Write

10 scooters

Trace the word **ten.**

Draw **ten** airplanes in the sky.

Trace and write the numbers 11 to 20.

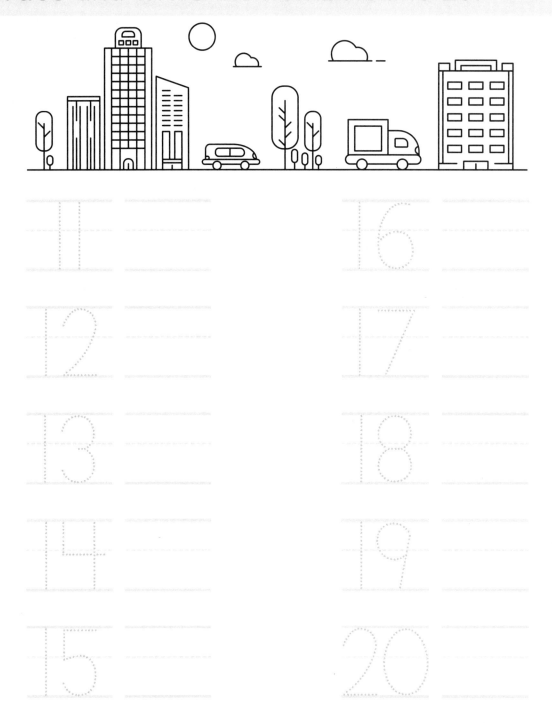

11

2

3

4

5

6

7

8

9

20

Chapter 5

One-to-One Correspondence

Color the vehicles showing 3 of their wheels.

The Cars, Trucks, Trains, and Planes Pre-K Workbook

Match the number of wheels you can see on each vehicle with the correct numeral.

2

4

3

5

Draw 2 wheels on the excavator to help it keep working.

The Cars, Trucks, Trains, and Planes Pre-K Workbook

Count how many airplanes are in the air.

_____ airplanes

Count how many cities the airplane visits.

 cities

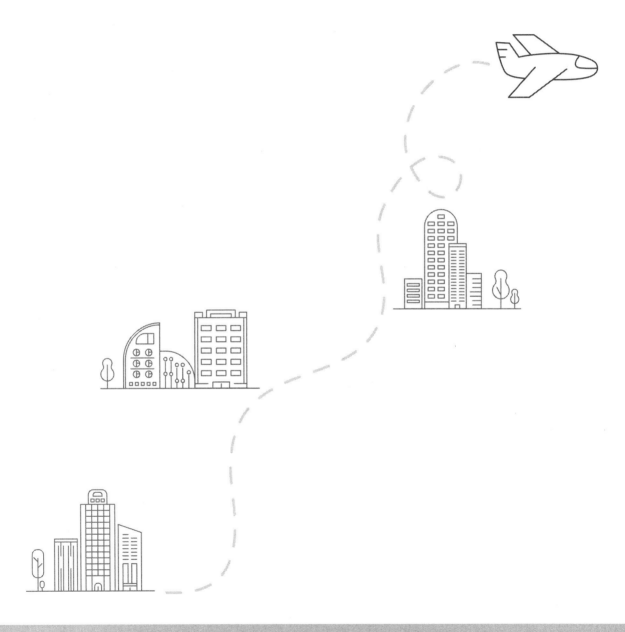

Color three of the train's windows blue and three of them red.

Count how many windows there are on the train in all.

_____ windows

Count how many race cars are in the race.

_____ race cars

The Cars, Trucks, Trains, and Planes Pre-K Workbook

Color four of your favorite vehicles.

SCHOOL BUS

Count how many waves it will take for the boat to reach the lighthouse.

_____ waves

Color 5 of the wheels on the emergency vehicles.

Chapter 6

Shape Tracing and Identification

Circle

Trace the circle below. Start at the airplane and end at the dot.

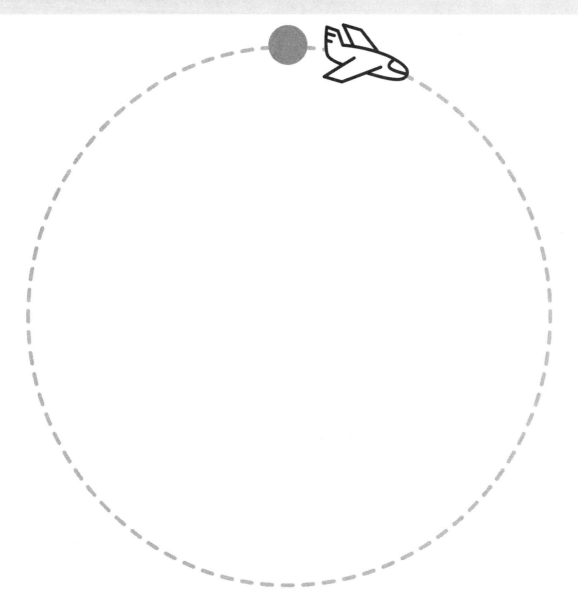

Color the pictures that have circles.

Square

Trace the square below. Start at the car and end at the dot.

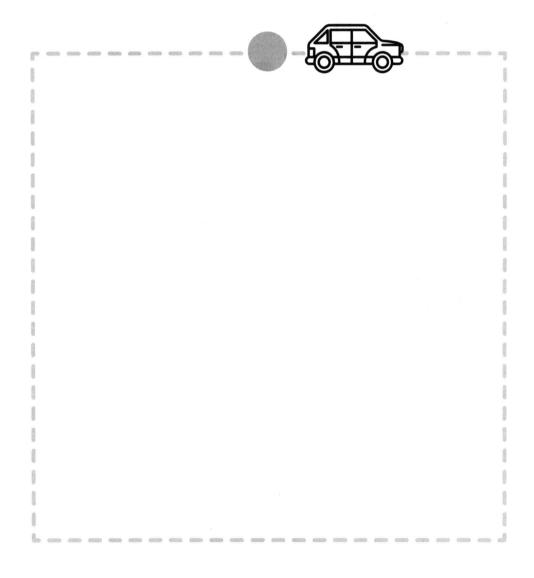

The Cars, Trucks, Trains, and Planes Pre-K Workbook

Trace all seven squares below to help the construction workers finish the building.

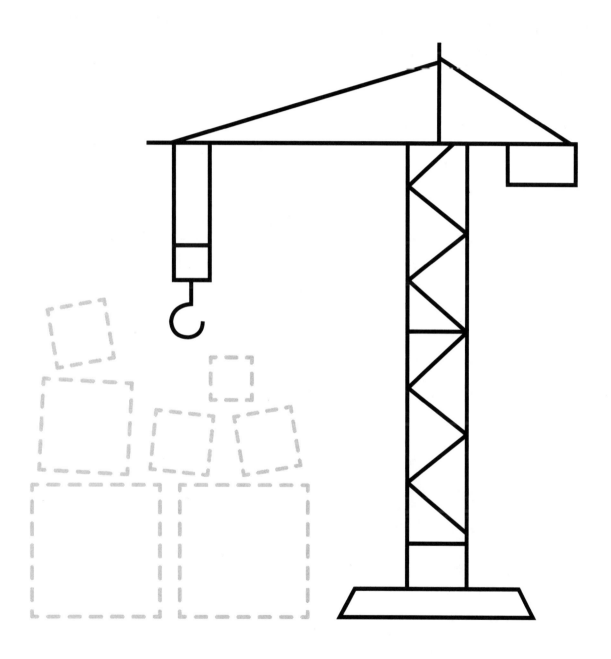

Triangle

Trace the triangle below. Start at the train engine and end at the dot.

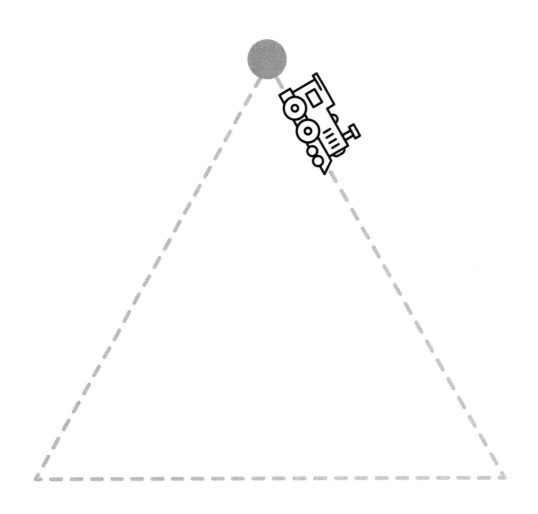

Trace and **color** in the triangles below to help keep the load in the dump truck.

Build a triangle by putting together all three sides.

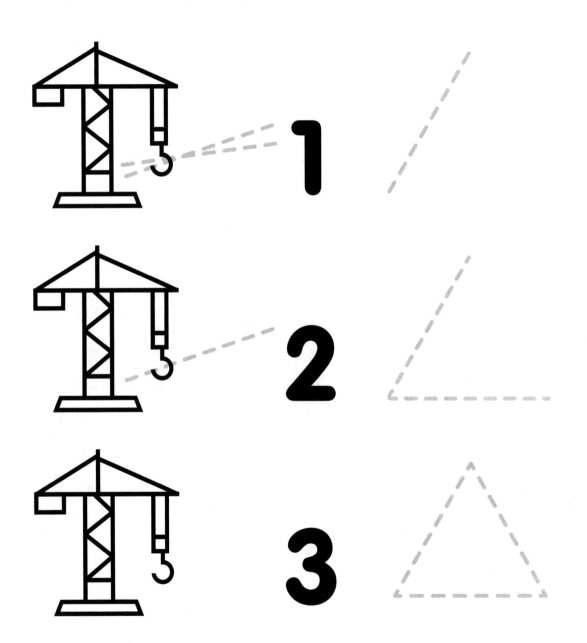

The Cars, Trucks, Trains, and Planes Pre-K Workbook

Rectangle

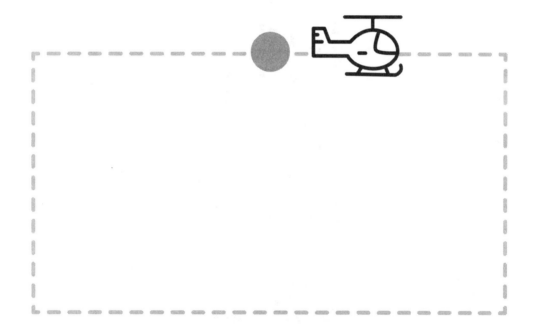

Draw a rectangle building to finish the city.

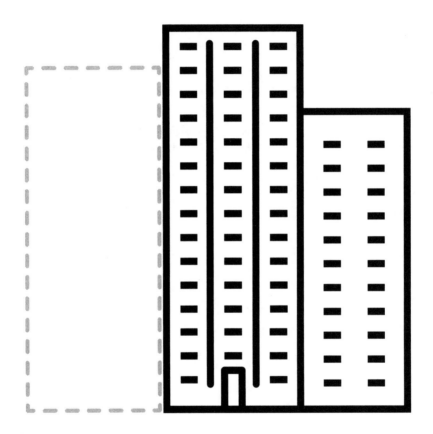

The Cars, Trucks, Trains, and Planes Pre-K Workbook

Oval

Trace the oval below. Start at the airplane and end at the dot.

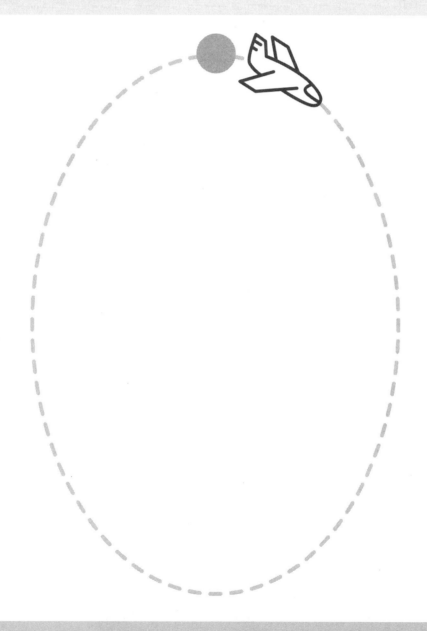

Star

Trace the star below. Start at the scooter and end at the dot.

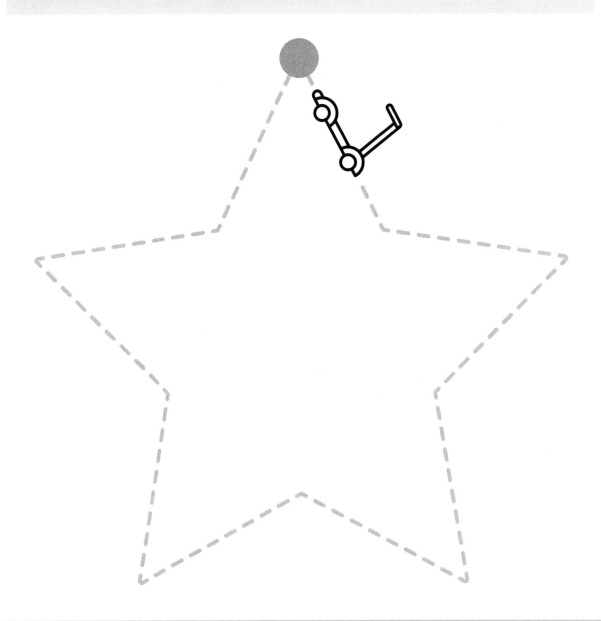

The Cars, Trucks, Trains, and Planes Pre-K Workbook

Shapes

Trace and **color** in the shapes below to make a special vehicle.

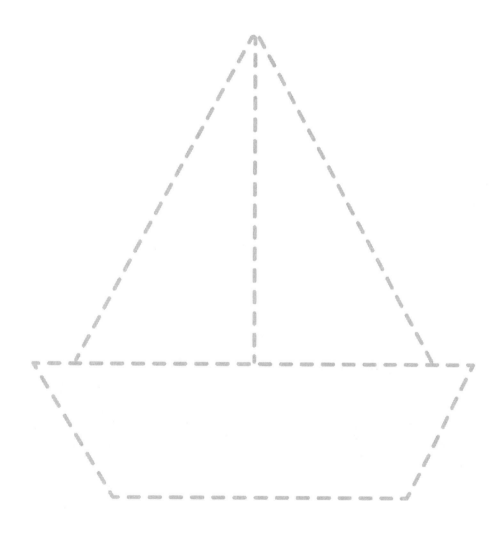

Shapes

Trace and **color** only the circles so they can be unloaded at the station.

Shapes

Trace and **color** only the rectangles so the dump truck can move them from the work site.

Shapes

Draw two circles to complete the car.

Draw five squares on the empty building to create windows.

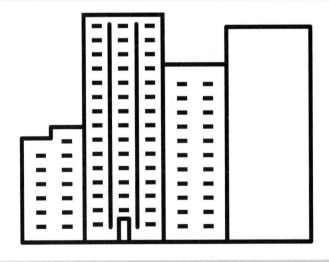

The Cars, Trucks, Trains, and Planes Pre-K Workbook

Chapter 7

Matching Similar Objects

Pair the uppercase letters with their lowercase letters by drawing a line between the matching dump trucks.

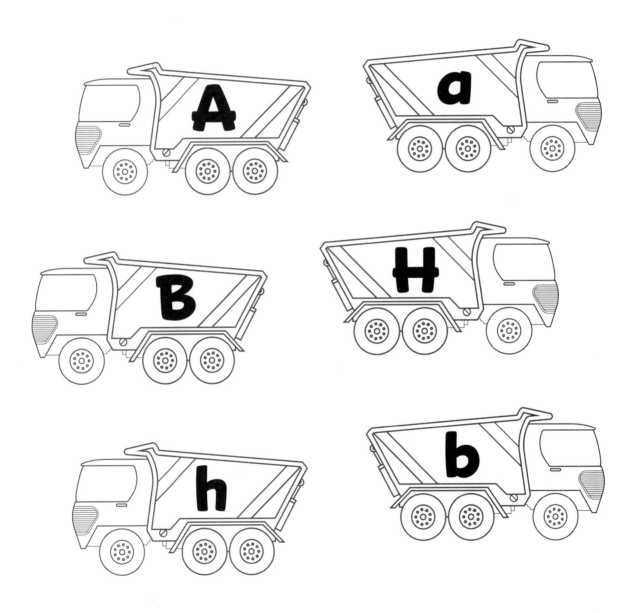

The Cars, Trucks, Trains, and Planes Pre-K Workbook

Draw lines to match the pictures that are the same.

Circle the pictures that are the same.

Draw a line to match the two cities that have the same numbers of cars on the road.

Circle the vehicles that have the same number of wheels.

Draw more train cars on the bottom train so that it matches the train on top.

Draw lines to connect the locomotives with matching lowercase and uppercase letters.

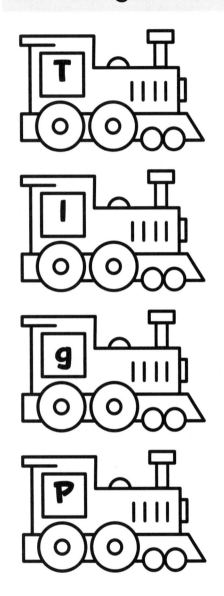

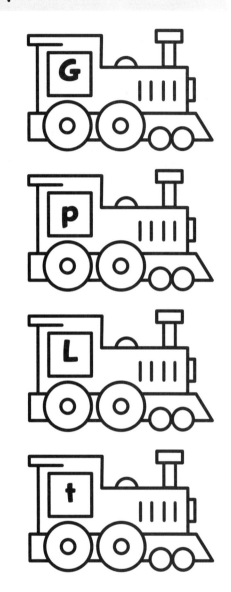

The Cars, Trucks, Trains, and Planes Pre-K Workbook

Circle the cement trucks that have the same driver.

Draw lines to match the crane trucks with the same shapes.

The Cars, Trucks, Trains, and Planes Pre-K Workbook

Circle the vehicles driving in the same spot.
Color the cars.

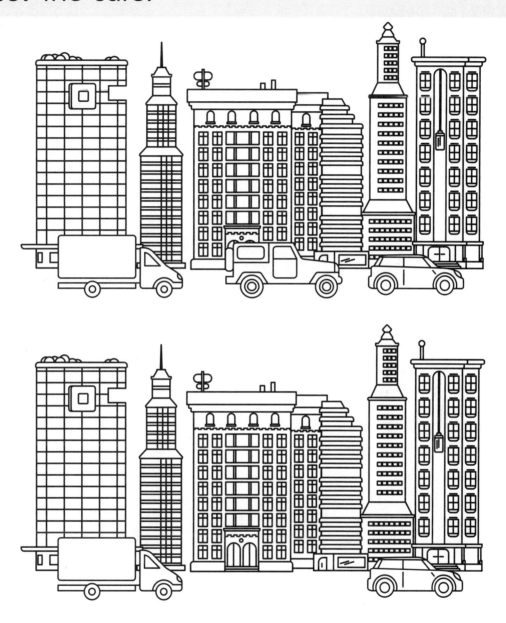

Chapter **8**

Following Directions

Circle the vehicles on the ground. Draw a square around the vehicles in the sky.

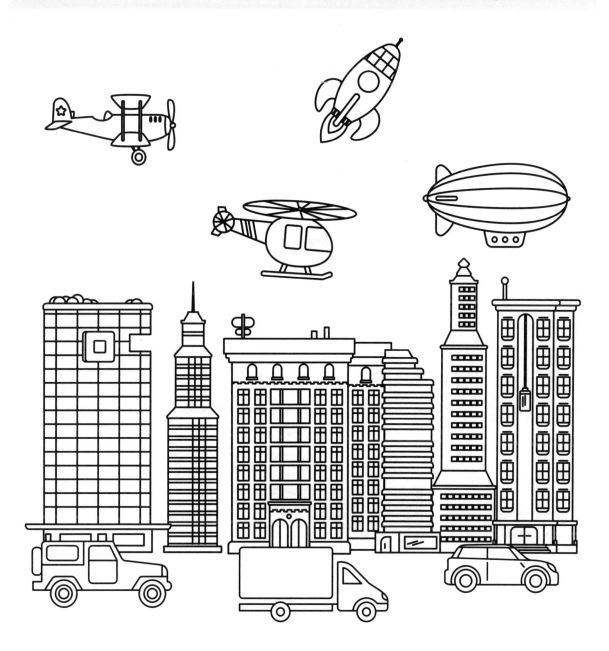

Find the path that takes the construction worker to her site.

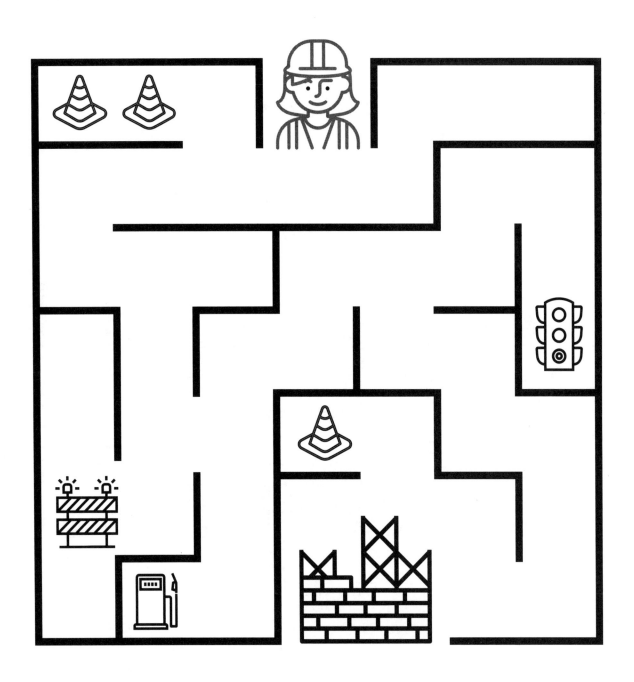

The Cars, Trucks, Trains, and Planes Pre-K Workbook

Circle the airplanes that are flying toward the **right**.

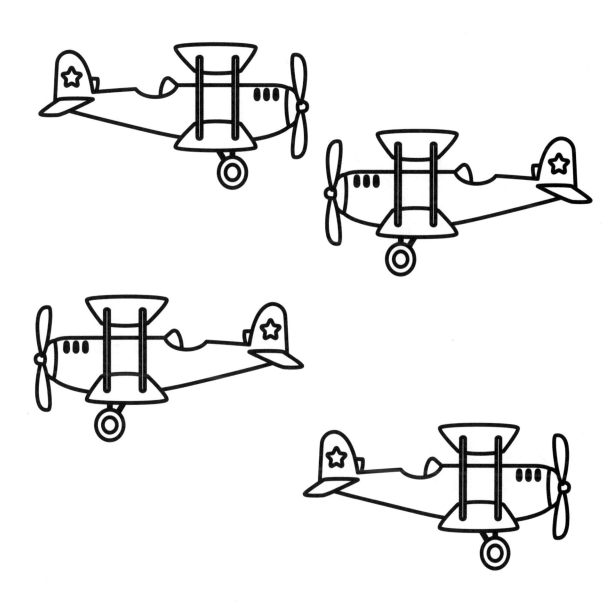

Circle the helicopters that are flying **above** the mountains.

The Cars, Trucks, Trains, and Planes Pre-K Workbook

Draw a **square** around the cars that are driving to the left.

Circle the vehicles that are to the **right** of the trees.

Draw a **square** around the vehicles flying above the birds.

Color the vehicles that are right side up.

Trace the right line to get the police car to the city.

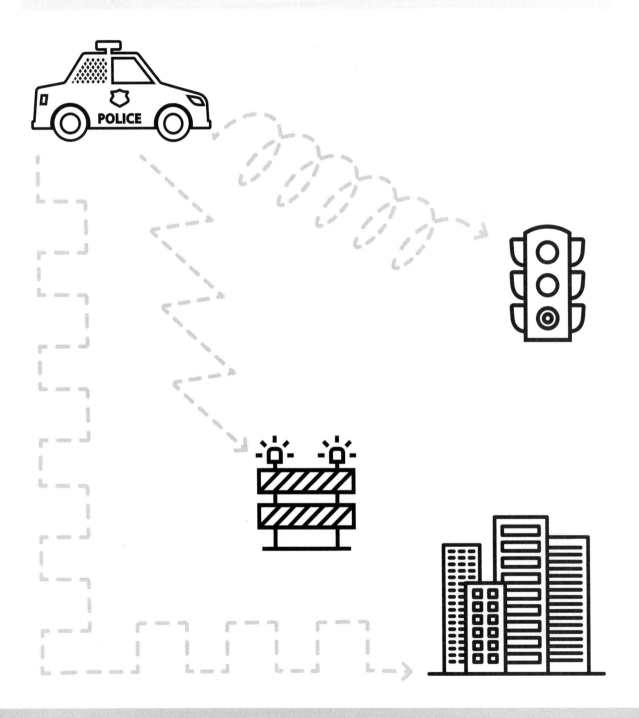

The Cars, Trucks, Trains, and Planes Pre-K Workbook

Draw a **square** around the car that is in the front of the race.

Help the race car make it to the finish line.

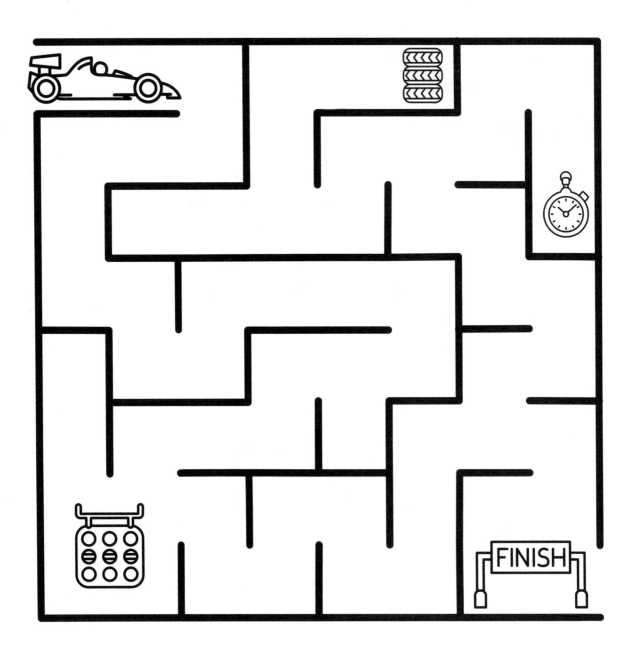

The Cars, Trucks, Trains, and Planes Pre-K Workbook

Chapter 9

Finding Same and Different Items

Color the airplanes red. Color the helicopters blue.

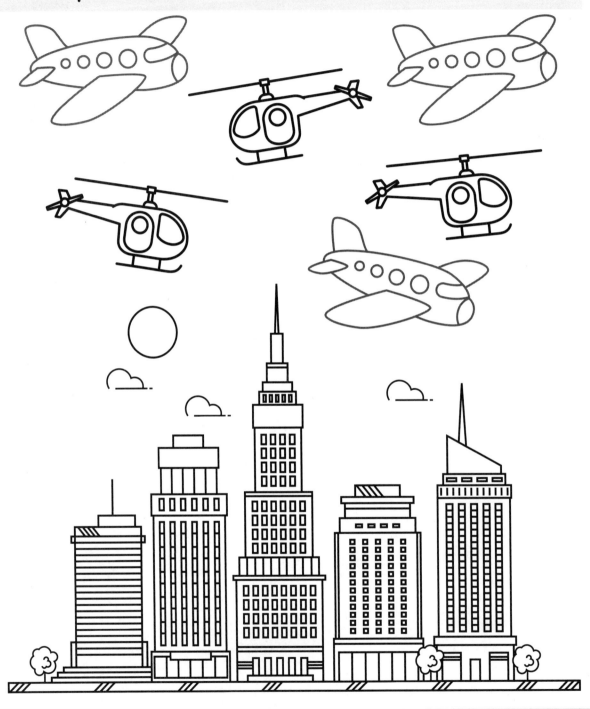

The Cars, Trucks, Trains, and Planes Pre-K Workbook

Color the vehicle that is different in each row.

Circle the vehicles that are the same size in each row.

The Cars, Trucks, Trains, and Planes Pre-K Workbook

Color the vehicles that are facing the same way in each row.

Spot the difference. Draw a circle around it.

Circle the vehicles with the same number of wheels in each row.

Circle the 3 differences in the construction sites.

The Cars, Trucks, Trains, and Planes Pre-K Workbook

Circle the boats that are the same in each row.

Color the jets that are facing the same direction in each picture.

The Cars, Trucks, Trains, and Planes Pre-K Workbook

Circle the 5 differences in the cities.

 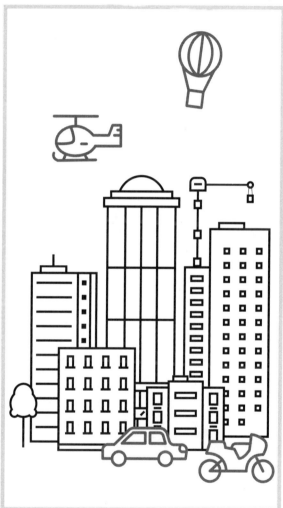

Tracing Vocabulary Words

Shapes

square

circle

triangle

rectangle

Directions

up

down

left

right

Actions

draw

trace

spot

color